CHAPTER 1

STYLES IN EVERY DIRECTION

Everyone knows that Harry began his career in One Direction . . . or did he?! The name of his first band is super ironic considering the charmed career of charming Harry Styles—because in addition to skyrocketing, his career has gone in many directions!

When Harry first appeared on *The X Factor*, he was voted off! Can you even? He was only sixteen years old and auditioned at Manchester Central. He sang an enchanting rendition of Stevie Wonder's "Isn't She Lovely," which judge Nicole Scherzinger loved. But another judge, Louis Walsh, didn't think he was ready for the big-time competition. So he was sent to boot camp, and still he failed to qualify for the "Boys" category.

D1403146

But guess who else also failed?

One hundred percent correct: Liam Payne, Louis Tomlinson, Niall Horan, and Zayn Malik.

The mind reels. We've all seen the clip of Harry's audition. He rocked it. His charm beams through the camera, and his voice is practically perfect. To not even get a spot? What were they thinking? Or was it all a ruse to keep viewers tuned in until they sorted out exactly what to do with these five adorbs guys who were clearly talented out the wazoo?

Here's the thing of it: Have you ever played a game of Simon Says? And wondered who the heck was Simon that he got to tell everyone what to do? Us too.

HERE'S THE SCOOP!

↓ ON SIMON SAYS! ↓

★ The game Simon Says is centuries old.

★ How old? Well, the saying was originally "Cicero dicit fac hoc"—Latin for "Cicero says do this."

★ In ancient Rome, it was in your best interest to do what statesman Marcus Tullius Cicero told you to do.

★ It changed to "Simon" when a thirteenth-century French-English nobleman named Simon de Montfort got so much power that he even put King Henry III in prison.

By now, you're probably wondering why in the world we're bringing this up, as the Simon of *The X Factor* was born centuries after the playground game became a thang. But trust us as we throw back to the twenty-first century to tell you there's a reason Simon Cowell *is* Simon Cowell. And we should all do what he says because the man knows his business! Although the boys didn't progress as solo acts, Simon says (see what we did there?), "It was really weird. I just said, 'Why don't we put these guys into a group?' It took ten minutes!" Rightly, Simon thought they were "too talented to let go of."

But wait! We have SCOOP! drama! Was it Simon Cowell or Nicole Scherzinger who had the idea to put them together?!?! They both make that claim to fame! We already know that Simon said it took him ten minutes to realize they were perfect for forming a group, but Nicole says it was her idea. "I just thought: 'Wow, these boys! None of them were strong enough to make [it] through, but they'd make a killer group,'" Nicole said. Then she added quite the endnote: "I think they said the footage of me suggesting it mysteriously disappeared."

Well, we're not going to quibble about exactly who said it first, because anyone who took one look at that group of guys could tell they would knock it out of the park.

It was Harry who came up with the idea to name the group One Direction, naturally. He was also the one who came up with the name for his high school band, White Eskimo. He's just that kind of guy, you know? Wit, charm, and lots of good energy have brought Mr. Styles far. It's as if he was born with those qualities. In fact, his mum, Anne, fessed up that, "Ever since he was young he's made people smile. I always thought he'd end up on the stage."

What's hard to believe is that during their first year on *The X Factor,* One Direction came in third behind Rebecca Ferguson and Matt Cardle.

What's *NOT* hard to believe is that the 1D boys were the life and soul of *The X Factor* that season! Sources say the boys were always up to something, one off hiding in a cupboard, another off trying on clothes, full of hijinks and fun. Of course, Harry stood out as the star and was adored by all.

Here's the **SCOOP!** on Harry. The 1D boys all shared a house the year they were on the show. The first night they moved in was mellow. They played music and Ping-Pong with lots of room downstairs, but the sleeping quarters were tight! Each band member had some interesting quirks the others had to get used to. LOL. For example, Louis was extremely messy, and our dear Hazza not only snored but talked in his sleep! We wish they'd been recording because we'd love to know what he had to say.

Even though 1D came in third place, Simon Cowell called them to his office and offered them a $2 million recording contract with Syco Music in December 2010. Interesting that first-place winner Cardle was only offered a $1 million contract. Again, listen to what Simon says. He knows the international market!

We know that you know what happened from here, but it's too awesome not to recap!

Simon brought these five young men to the US, and they began recording with producer RedOne.

The anticipation for their first music video reached fever pitch because initially only the lyrics for their debut song, "What Makes You Beautiful," were released on YouTube. The group filmed the corresponding video in Malibu, and they teased its release with each member of the group having his chance to announce how many days were left until it dropped. And when it did come out? Mayhem!

Watching Niall, Liam, Louis, Zayn, and of course Harry frolic at a fun day on the beach is like stepping into a dreamscape, compliments of an American Eagle ad. We immediately want to jump through the screen and join them! It's absolutely amazing! Between the five of them, there's something that appeals to everyone, and to top it off, they're singing all the right things about how girls are beautiful without makeup and encouraging them to be confident. There's no downside here. And it's Harry who has the romantic moment where he sings sweetly to a pretty brunette who looks clearly smitten. Can you blame her?

You could tell 1D genuinely had fun together. So much so that they broke the record for pre-album sales at Sony and "WMYB" hit number one on the UK charts. See? Simon says!

That debut single was part of their first album, *Up All Night*. It was the UK's fastest-selling album of 2011, and before you knew it, the boys were off on tour. They went on the *Today* show—you know the one, where fans gather behind a glass wall in the background and scream like banshees? Well, for Harry and the boys, fifteen thousand of those banshees descended upon Rockefeller Center. Complete chaos. But fun chaos.

Simon marketed it perfectly: He had both Kelly Clarkson and Ed Sheeran write songs for the album. Lo and behold, One Direction set a Guinness World Record as the first band from Britain to have their debut album reach number one in the US.

They went on to win the Brit Awards best single in 2012, and they were shook. Up till that moment, a certain someone had been collecting lots of awards, a someone of whom Harry is a huge fan. Adele! They couldn't believe they won anything during her streak.

1D even performed "What Makes You Beautiful" at the 2012 London Olympics closing ceremony.

They were now pop royalty, but they were still normal boys who got homesick on tour and liked to lighten the load with some shenanigans, or as we like to call them, Harranigans—that's our word for Harry when he's a "scamp"! ("Scamp" is British slang for a child who's up to no good.)

"We've all been having a lot of fun in the dressing rooms, getting up to mischief. Liam was asleep and Zayn shaved a slit in his eyebrow and I shaved my initials into his leg hair."

The fun 1D had together bounded through the screen in their videos: the aforementioned day outside, hopping through London like a mini John, Paul, George, Ringo, and Pete Best (hints of things to come, we guess) on the red double-decker buses. The guys were flying the British flag, a huge part of their appeal.

One Directioners were at a fever pitch waiting for the second album. Have you ever heard of the sophomore slump? It applies to almost everything—the second year of college, or phase two of a new job, meaning everyone expected the band to rush their second album and ruin it because the fans were so rabid for the next round.

But *Take Me Home* did anything but slump à la

sophomore. It was more like a slam, debuting on the very top of the UK Albums Chart and becoming the second-fastest-selling album of 2012.

They kept it very Brit with the album cover featuring the 1D boys in, out, and on top of a fabulous royal-red phone box.

The lead single, "Live While We're Young," is totally "'80s-inflected and intermittently rock-dappled," and not your typical boy-band pop. But the reception to the track was indeed typical of the 1D fans! Understandably.

The video is to die for. Niall, Louis, Zayn, Liam, and our Harry look to be having a blast in a day at a campground after waking up, seemingly unsure how they got there. But they make the most of it in their unique way. There's something very special about the self-aware charm of young guys (and girls) who aren't afraid to make fun of themselves—a priceless skill no matter one's age.

They have fun on the lake, get soaked by water guns, lose at soccer, get thrown in the pool, and generally live it up. Their friendship is evident.

The guys were having a blast living and working together, almost like five best friends at school, except they were making platinum albums and had hordes of screaming fans.

Yet there's always more Harry **SCOOP!** Even though Harry had made it clear he wanted things to remain absolutely even and fair between all the guys, it was obvious Harry was emerging as the leader of the group. He's such fun, and everyone gravitates toward him. He has that je ne sais quoi, that savoir faire, and that thing one loves but can't quite put one's finger on— otherwise known as dimples.

We jest! But Harry and his Harranigans made people take note. He was gregarious and fun, and not just with the fans, but other musicians, too! Ed

Sheeran told Xfm that "Harry's a lad—I was with him last night actually. Being in music you're quite segregated from everyone and you're always busy doing promo. When you're on the same promo run as someone or in the same kind of situation as someone you grow quite close, friendship-wise. He's a very cool guy."

One Direction continued as a group of equals in name. During the summer of 2013, they released their third album, *Midnight Memories*, as well as a documentary and concert film called *One Direction: This Is Us*. Naturally, the film topped both the UK and US box offices, and the tickets for the *Where We Are* tour sold out in minutes.

Things were moving at lightning speed, so fast that some were worried for the 1D guys. "I've never known a band to announce a second summer tour before the first tour is over. It's insane–they're working them like dogs," said Andy Greene, an editor with *Rolling Stone*.

Indeed, they were only going to get four or five

days off a month on the tour, and it was a kicker. Fans were worried they would burn out, but the guys kept the flame and Harranigans going. They started #PiersMorganIsSmelly trending worldwide on Twitter after Piers Morgan, the British broadcaster, criticized their hero David Beckham. We understand their standing up for David, but we hope they also understand that Piers Morgan criticizes nearly everyone, so they might've found themselves defending the world if they had kept it up!

Now that Harry and the guys were global superstars, you wouldn't be crazy to think things would go to their heads and they'd become just another rock group, trashing hotels and being full of themselves. But nope.

WE HAVE CHARITABLE SCOOP!

One Direction had been involved with Children in Need since 2011, and in 2013 they released the cover single "One Way or Another," with proceeds going to Comic Relief. They performed at the Pride of Britain Awards (honoring Brits who have displayed extraordinary bravery or courage in harrowing situations) as well as the 2014 Royal Variety Performance (supports entertainers who are sick, elderly, or impoverished) with the Duke and Duchess of Cambridge in attendance. Niall Horan raised money for Irish Autism Action, and then in 2013, Liam and our Harry partnered with Trekstock, which raises funds for cancer research. They auctioned off an evening out with the duo in exchange for a donation, and natch, they went above their goal of $500,000. The #HangwithLiam&Harry global campaign raised $784,984, which allowed Trekstock to completely fund their Hodgkin's lymphoma trial. Well done, guys!!!

CHAPTER 2

GOING SOLO?

By now, it was clear: One Direction was here to stay. *Or were they?*

Next up was the album *Midnight Memories*, debuting at number one in the UK and US in November 2013. The music was a little edgier, and it featured songs written by Niall, Liam, and Harry. We know Harry looked up to musicians like Chris Martin and his band Coldplay, so it's not surprising he was ready to change 1D's sound. But it's also not surprising that with such a tight schedule, cracks would form in the seemingly perfect world of One Direction.

Harry and the guys toured *Midnight Memories* and its hit single, "Best Song Ever," with the *Where We Are* tour beginning in April 2014, also releasing

One Direction: Where We Are—The Concert Film.

Believe it or not, they then announced their fourth album, *Four,* by September 2014.

That schedule? Pure madness! We totes understand that it eventually got to them. Even though videos such as "Best Song Ever," where they raided some film honcho's office, are hilarious, fun, and works of art that could be studied by future film students, there's a catch. They hint to the boys' growing dissatisfaction at being in a boy band at the beck and call of executives mostly concerned with the bottom line.

Harry later said, "I wasn't one hundred percent behind the music. It wasn't me. It was music that was already given to us, and we were told 'this is what is going to sell to these people.' As much as we were the biggest, most famous boy band in the world, it felt weird."

Hazza wasn't the only one feeling weird. Less than two months into *Four*'s *On the Road Again* tour, One Direction announced Zayn Malik's departure.

The fans and Twitter went wild, posting everything from "VANESSA JUST CALLED ME CRYING IN SCHOOL SHES IN A BATHROOM STALL CRYING ABOUT HOW ZAYN LEFT SHES CALLING HER MOM TO PICK HER UP I FEEL BAD" to "zayn malik took the name of the album 'FOUR' way too seriously" to our favorite, "It could be worse. It could be Harry."

Hear! Hear!

Well, Dear Harry stayed on, and One Direction made their first appearance as a group of four on *The Late Late Show with James Corden*—the host is a great friend of Harry's. They played tattoo roulette, and of course, Harry lost and had to get "Late Late" permanently inked on his arm. Always good-natured and easygoing, he didn't seem to mind too much. But his bromance with Corden must've made the whole scenario a bit easier!

One Direction released one more album, *Made in the A.M.*, with hits like "Drag Me Down," and topped the charts once again. The video for "Drag

Me Down" seemed to be yet another hint, with the guys portrayed as astronauts in training who are later jettisoned into space—perhaps proving they could still skyrocket up the charts. But maybe considering recent troubles, things felt a wee bit alien? Despite proving they could succeed as a foursome, One Direction soon announced they would be going on hiatus.

As we know, that hiatus has lasted indefinitely.

Our Harry didn't waste any time, though, and within months he launched his own label, Erskine Records, and signed again with Columbia, who had been part of 1D's label along with Syco. Hazza's single "Sign of the Times" was number one on the UK Singles Chart. The video is to die for, with Harry flying through the air and walking on water in Scotland's Isle of Skye.

Natch, we have Harranigan SCOOP! In the video for "Sign of the Times," Harry actually dangled from one helicopter while being filmed from another helicopter. Literally cloud cuckoo

23

land. We guess he wasn't kidding when he spoke about venturing out on his own: "I think it was time for me to be scared. And I'm having the time of my life working this out."

The song itself is just divine, very glam and reminiscent of David Bowie. Harry has a great solo sound, and even though we're huge 1D fans, it's like Hazza has come into his own. The vid ends with him floating up into the stratosphere, a fitting metaphor as Harry is destined for the stars.

The album was eponymously titled *Harry Styles*, a brilliant move. The name alone has everyone charmed, and it seemed Harry was always the one best suited for a solo career. As you know, we always follow what Simon says. He laid it bare: "I would say you're drawn to Harry's personality. He's very charming and seems to be the one person who would be easiest to talk to."

Harry was suited and booted for sure, and the album debuted at number one in the US, UK, and Down Under.

And here's the **SCOOP!** on Harry's tours! *Harry Styles: Live on Tour* sold out in seconds, so we can say the fans love him, plus he loves them back and treats them with such courtesy. When Harry played San Jose, he saw a fan's sign reading: "I'm Gonna Come Out to My Parents Because of You!" After asking her name and her mum's name, he shouts it out to her mum. Then he wrangles the entire stadium into shouting, "Tina [the mum], she's [Grace, the daughter] gay," and it was a stunningly lovely way to help a fan who wanted to come out! Then he sang "What Makes You Beautiful." A knight in shining armor if we've ever seen one. Happy tears! Squish!

The fans weren't the only ones in thrall, because the critical reception was *beyond*! Check out the headlines: "Ending a year-long classic arena tour, Harry Styles proves he is the future of rock 'n' roll." "Solo show finds Harry Styles heading in the right direction." "'Harry Styles: Live on Tour' showcases the superstar's skills and swagger." You would think Harry would be heading only in One Direction, no?

No!! Just as it looked like Hazza was only a music man, he added a few more pieces to his repertoire. He put on his acting cap! Surely you know he starred in *Dunkirk*, which we will get into, but did you know he also appeared on the TV series *iCarly*? He was adorable as ever, playing himself and unable to perform a big show due to a case of "jungle worms" he'd caught drinking from the title character's bottle. He drips with charm as he continues to play sick so that Carly will continue to care for him, offering a magnetism and natural charisma that jumps through the screen.

He's an absolute natural, evident in a hilarious sketch on *Saturday Night Live* when 1D were the musical guests. Harry crossed the artistry lines beautifully when he performed a spot-on Mick Jagger (lead singer of the Rolling Stones) in a "Celebrity Family Feud: Time Travel Edition" sketch. He nailed all the inimitable Mick mannerisms from the openmouthed pout, popping his tongue out from time to time, and standing like a jittery peacock about to strut off! He even sounded like him, with the barely-enunciated Cockney words snapping out of his mouth in mangled hilarity.

Harry's ease in front of the camera shone further when he hosted *The Late Late Show with James Corden* during the period when James's wife was giving birth. He didn't miss a beat delivering the monologue—a much harder feat than it looks. Standing alone in front of a live audience and delivering jokes can go wrong. Stony silences. Heckling. Booing. But Harry had them wrapped around his little finger and hit every note perfectly. Pun 100 percent intended.

Now for our *Dunkirk* SCOOP! Director Christopher Nolan had NO IDEA about Harry's rock superstardom until he cast him in the role of Allied soldier Alex. "I don't think I was that aware really of how famous Harry was," Nolan said. "I mean, my daughter had talked about him. My kids talked about him, but I wasn't really that aware of it. So the truth is, I cast Harry because he fit the part wonderfully and truly earned a seat at the table."

Not only did Hazza win the role on his own merits, but he beat out hundreds of other actors, some of whom had training at prestigious schools. And he did that on top of his fame actually being a detriment! "Our aim was to have people who are fresh and don't bring a lot of prior work with them, so the audience will be really immersed in the film and not struggling with recognizable famous personalities," said casting director John Papsidera. "So, Harry really had to overcome hurdles to get past that. He fought hard for it and his work was impressive and that's what attracted us to him."

Reporters and journalists agreed that his work was indeed impressive, noting that Styles gave "an impressive debut performance"! *The Hollywood Reporter* noted that "Harry Styles has emerged as a secret weapon for Christopher Nolan's *Dunkirk*." And *Vulture* wrote that he's "the one driving the action during the film's most gripping scene . . . and the guy's just got a spark to him." Tell us something we don't know!

We couldn't blame Dear Harry if he just went full-throttle thespian and solely pursued acting, as it seems he would head straight for an Oscar. But Hazza does anything but go in One Direction. Like a true artist, he loves exploring many avenues of creativity, and we wouldn't be surprised if he ended up writing a novel or painting a canvas that ended up in the Louvre.

If anyone could walk that Fine Line (last pun, we promise!) between artistries, it would be Harry. But don't forget, Harry is a scamp. And he does the unexpected. What he did was walk right back to music—writing songs and working in the studio, which brings us to now.

Harry's incredible second solo album, *Fine Line*, came out in December 2019, and we were just blown away. We talked about how his first solo album was very David Bowie–like, and for *Fine Line*, Harry no doubt dove even deeper into '70s–inspired rock, as well as much of the latter half of the twentieth century. In this incredible mix, we can hear traces of Bowie along with the Beatles; Pink Floyd; Crosby, Stills, Nash, & Young; the Rolling Stones; and even Fleetwood Mac.

The feels are so intense with Fleetwood Mac that we have another small SCOOP! for you. Harry loves their music so much that he became good friends with F-Mac legend Stevie Nicks, even giving a tribute when she was inducted into the Rock & Roll Hall

of Fame. "She's always there for you. She knows what you need: advice, a little wisdom, a blouse, a shawl." In return? Ms. Nicks accidentally called Harry's former band *NSync. Lots of rockers would go ballistic at that! But Dear Harry? He took it in stride with a dimpled smile and easygoing grace. And that is why we love him.

Fine Line is full of romance (SCOOP! more on his inspiration in Chapter 4!), with singles like "Adore You" and "Watermelon Sugar," and lyrics like "I'd walk through fire for you" and "Baby, you're the end of June." And we are full of admiration. As is the *New York Times*, which wrote one of the best reviews ever of *Fine Line*: "a production tour-de-force . . . shimmering brilliance and voices stack up in surreal stereo fireworks . . . gorgeous patience, eventually summoning an orchestra. Free of his boy band, Styles exults in sound, not image."

While we are thrilled for Dear Harry to have gotten great reviews, don't dismiss that image quite yet because we are beside ourselves to see it during the *Love On Tour.*

Next up, we're going to splash out with a full investigation into what's behind that image and everything that makes Harry the loveliest, cheekiest, most caring scamp in rock and roll.

CHAPTER 3

LIFE STYLES

*H*arry has tons of style, which is screamingly obvious by now. But you know there are many different kinds of style. While we're going to deep dive into DH's (Dear Harry's) musical and sartorial style ("sartorial" is a fancy word for fashion), we'll more importantly look at his personal lifestyle since it's what's on the inside that makes him unique. Rarely does someone come on the scene with both talent and such ease with themself as a person. Often the uber-talented have an understandable self-consciousness, which comes from sensitivity. Those who feel deeply are often the ones able to translate their experiences into art. What makes DH ridiculously, extremely special is that he not only has a profoundly emotional makeup but also natural ease, spark, and the ability to see the best in people and things. This also makes him especially wise. He understands how to both enjoy and be productive in life—something many people don't achieve until later years, if ever!

So, how did he get that way? Nature and nurture. Let's start at the beginning.

Harry was born February 1, 1994 (an Aquarius— aka the friends of the world, natch), to Anne Cox and Desmond Styles, and has an older sister (by three years), Gemma. They started in Worcestershire but then made their home in Holmes Chapel, Cheshire. His mum explained, "I always thought he'd end up on the stage." Sister Gemma agrees.

Gemma wrote an article about Harry for *Another Man* and explained that even when he was too young for school, he would accompany her on car rides, and he "would be stood up in the back of the car, entertaining everyone through the open window. Even then he had that sort of magnetism that made people just want to watch him. He made people laugh. Babies still tend to stare at him now."

But don't think everything was smooth sailing and that DH didn't have some obstacles. His father sat him and Gemma down to tell them he was leaving when Harry was just seven. There were lots of tears. Harry was heartbroken. Unsurprisingly, DH is super close with his mum and sister, who clearly brought him up with exquisite manners and taught him to be kind. You can see it in everything he does.

SCOOP! CASE IN POINT!

We've looked at *quite* a bit of Hazza concert footage, and we can tell he retains his fun-loving spark and wit no matter what the crowd throws at him. *Literally!* Harry has gotten splashed with water and had flags and phones thrown onstage. And a water bottle once hit him! His responses, respectively, were to: enjoy the water fight and laugh while good-naturedly spraying the fans back; wrap the flag around his shoulders and dance, which made the audience deliriously happy; sweetly and laughingly convince the fan they'd need their phone back; and that last one . . . well, that hurt. But DH didn't get angry, or yell, or leave

> the stage. He didn't say a word. He crouched in pain until it passed, then went on as if nothing untoward had happened!!

We shall not name names, but there's another male rock star the same age as DH who doesn't have the same manners. In fact, his reactions to exactly the same things being thrown onstage were the opposite. Yelling, berating fans, stomping off the stage, and ending the show in a way that reminded us of a toddler throwing all their toys out of the pram.

The point here is not to humiliate that unnamed rock star because there are plenty of others who behave the same way. Our point is to illustrate what a solid personality Harry has.

His father: "He's just got this fantastic personable demeanor to him. Clearly he's a bit special."

His mother: "I know I'm his mum, but he really is a lovely young man and he's coming across exactly as he is at home."

So if you're thinking that of course his parents will say nice things but siblings are another story, here's Gemma: "His bundles of talent are a mixture of natural ability and intense heart."

Okay, okay, you're thinking that she's still his family. But then we have Simon Wakefield, owner of the bakery in Holmes Chapel where DH used to work before hitting the big-time: "[Harry] was the most polite member of staff we've ever had."

Harry's also not afraid to laugh at himself, one of the best personality traits ever. Hence his willingness to join James Corden in a *Late Late Show* sketch where the British men face off for a game of dodgeball against the USA ladies, who duly beat the pants off of them. (USA team captain was Michelle Obama; of course they won.) They did this hilarious bit about the difference between how the teams spent their halftime, with the US huddling into a rousing pep talk, but the UK being oh so British, sitting about quietly having tea, with Harry quipping, "Oh Benedict," when Mr. Cumberbatch says he thought it was supposed to be dogball.

But our favorite thing about Harry? He's kind.

A natural empath. DH stopped a concert to help a fan who was having a panic attack and had collapsed. He said into the mic, "Is everyone okay? You still with me? Do you want to help her up? If everyone could give her some space. If everyone could chill for one second, we'll get some people." Knight in shining armor.

Harry's kindness is the real thing, not just an affectation for his image! This guy is naturally a good person. It's a lifestyle! He is a dimpled, sweet, and hilarious young man. That's why no one can take their eyes off him—he's enchanting inside and out!

Since we're mentioning outer style, it's time to go sartorial. Harry's become known for his bold choices. He didn't start out that way, though. His debut on *The X Factor* saw him in a fairly tame gray cardigan and scarf, even though he always had the wild rocker curls. As his wardrobe grew, so did his hair, and at one point he had long, flowing locks to complement the skinny jeans and boots. Sometimes there were Beatles-esque suits. Hazza became more and more comfortable experimenting with his look, which is lucky for us because it's been a blast to watch the evolution. But don't let the fact that he thought about his clothes make you think he took things too seriously. Not our Harry!

SARTORIAL SCOOP!

DH was on Nick Grimshaw's Radio 1 show and claimed to borrow his sister Gemma's crotchless tights all the time. That he, in fact, wanted some of his own but wasn't sure if he should wear them out. He called his stylist, Caroline, while on the air, saying, "Basically, it just feels really comfortable, so I've been putting them on under my jeans. So I'm just wondering if you could get me some good ones. Like, some crotchless ones. Just because I've been stealing my sister's. The thing is, I'm not sure if I'm ready to bring them out. Maybe I should just keep them under my trousers for a bit. Do you think they do, like, gold ones?" He let poor Caroline scamper about a bit looking for tights!

The thing is, he was ready to let everyone think what they would before letting them in on the joke. He isn't afraid to experiment and supports everyone in their choices as well.

Unsurprisingly, his outfits have gotten further and further glam and bold, especially after going solo. He's not afraid to wear pink suits and heightened heels, or floral shirts and flared pinstripe trousers. He's even quoted Paul Simonon from the Clash: "Pink is the only true rock and roll color."

We love it! He also single-handedly brought pearl necklaces back in vogue after wearing one throughout his *Fine Line* promotions. They're not just for grandparents anymore. Since Harry's pearly presentation, Gigi Hadid has been seen sporting them around town, and the influencer site Popsugar even has a post titled "How to Wear the Pearl Necklace Trend for 2020." It's what to wear!

We've noticed a pattern, though. Lots of them, actually. But one of them in particular is the fact that his clothes have looked very '70s glam-rock, and that seems to be a huge era of musical influence for DH as well.

Hazza says Coldplay, Elvis, and the Beatles are musical heroes. We think it's easy to see their influence in some 1D songs like "End of the Day" (the Beatles' "A Day in the Life") and "Olivia" (the Beatles' "With a Little Help from My Friends"). Another similarity is how leading men in the respective groups clearly emerged. It's just that je ne *Styles* quoi, you know?

Going quickly backward (another direction), we think it's 100 percent Hazza how he handled the breakup of 1D. Zayn said things like he wouldn't listen to One Direction's music now, and that it was boringly generic. He also said he didn't make any friends while in the band.

We find that totes sad for Zayn, because look at how gracefully one can handle that situation, à la Hazza: "I know it's the thing that always happens. When somebody gets out of a band, they go, 'That wasn't me. I was held back.' But it was me. And I don't feel like I was held back at all. It was so much fun. If I didn't enjoy it, I wouldn't have done it. It's not like I was tied to a radiator." DH also added, "I think it's a shame [Zayn] felt that way. . . . I'm glad he's doing what he likes [now], and good luck to him." For his part, Harry says he kept those friendships from the band.

Now that, friends, is how you handle tough situations with grace. But that doesn't mean the transition from being in a group to becoming a solo artist was a complete breeze for Harry. In fact, he sought advice from someone who'd gone through the same transition . . .

Harry and former Beatles member Paul McCartney got on the horn in a sort of interview for *Another Man* magazine, and DH asked Paul point-blank, "When you first went from being in a band to being on your own, what was the creative side of that like?" Paul responded that he was thinking, "'Well, now what am I going to do, just make records that sound like the Beatles? Or, am I going to try and go in a completely different direction and do something that's really not like the Beatles?' So we started the group Wings, and then I just thought, 'Sod it, I'm going to write some stuff that I want to write and keep it away from what the Beatles might have done with it.'"

Worked for Paul, worked for Harry. Approach the masters, and you will learn! Learn Harry did, and this brings us back to our '70s influence, exactly when Paul McCartney went from the Beatles to Paul McCartney and Wings, writing absolute rockers like "Jet" and "Band on the Run."

Harry's first solo album laid out hits like "Sign of the Times," with sounds not dissimilar to Queen and Bowie. All very emotional music. Fans felt a huge intimacy with DH upon hearing the stunning "Sweet Creature," with its dreamy Fleetwood Mac–like guitar. That goes double for the song "Fine Line." At the launch concert, he wore large white David Bowie–ish flared pants and sang every song from the album. "Cherry" is folksy and sounds like it was recorded in Laurel Canyon in 1978, while "She" wouldn't sound out of place on a Pink Floyd album. *Rolling Stone* called Hazza a "Rock God and a Gentleman," and we couldn't agree more.

Harry's style is definitely that of a gentleman. Whether it's his clothes, his music, or the way he interacts with fans, Harry keeps it 100 percent. He just sends out good vibes. He told the crowd at that launch concert, "Please feel free to be whoever it is you want to be." DH is a true empath.

Before we move on to DH's love life, we want to leave you with a tiny gem.

GRATITUDE SCOOP!

A reporter who attended the launch concert noted that "if there was one fine line running through the entire event, it would have to be gratitude." Styles made it clear that he appreciated the turnout and his welcome return to the spotlight. Harry told the crowd, "I am so honored to be playing in front of you tonight. Truly. There is nothing that makes me more hopeful than standing in front of you. I thank you for that. You've completely changed my life. I love ya."

Harry loves performing, and he loves the world. We have news for him: The world loves him back!

SCOOP! QUIZ

HOW WELL DO YOU KNOW HAZZA?

How well do you know Hazza based on everything we've SCOOPed so far?

 ⬇ TAKE THIS QUIZ TO FIND OUT! ⬇

1. Harry runs into Zayn Malik at an awards show. What does he do?

A. IGNORE, IGNORE, IGNORE.

B. SHOOT HIM THE HAIRY EYEBALL AND THEN IGNORE.

C. GIVES HIM A SWEET SMILE AND WAVE, AND IF Z IS RECEPTIVE, RUNS OVER TO GIVE HIM A QUICK HUG.

D. TRIES TO BLOCK HIM OFF THE RED CARPET AND HOG ALL THE PHOTO OPS.

2. He can live in London, NYC, or LA. Where does he choose?

A. LA, DUDE. SUN AND FUN.

B. LONDON TOWN, TO BE NEAR THE FAM.

C. NYC, THE CITY THAT STAYS UP ALL NIGHT.

D. ALL OF THE ABOVE! IN FACT, HARRY HAS A PLACE IN ALL THREE!

3. Hazza slips and falls in front of thousands after a fan throws a flag onstage. What does he do?

A. GETS UP, LAUGHS, AND DRAPES THE FLAG AROUND HIS SHOULDERS TO DANCE.

B. YELLS AT THE FAN.

C. STOMPS OFFSTAGE.

D. RIPS IT TO SHREDS.

4. Harry has a night to himself. Does he . . .

A. GO SHOPPING?

B. GO OUT TO A BAR?

C. GO TO A SPORTING EVENT?

D. SIT DOWN AND LISTEN TO MUSIC, WRITING SOME HIMSELF?

5. He's on a first date and the girl is really rude to the waiter. What does he do?

A. LAUGHS.

B. LEADS BY BEING SUPER NICE HIMSELF BUT DOESN'T SHAME THE GIRL. LEAVES AN APOLOGY NOTE FOR THE WAITER AND AN EXTRA BIG TIP.

C. LOUDLY TELLS HER SHE NEEDS TO GET SOME MANNERS SO EVERYONE AROUND CAN HEAR.

D. JUST TURNS RED BUT FIGURES, WHATEVER, SHE'S PRETTY HOT.

6. Road trip with sister, Gemma, and mum, Anne! What do they do?

A. GO SOMEWHERE SUPER FANCY AND MUM AND SIS BARELY SEE HARRY, WHO PARTIES THE WHOLE TIME.

B. SOMEWHERE HE'S SURE TO BE SEEN BY FANS—HE CAN'T GO LONG WITHOUT THE ATTENTION.

C. NOWHERE. HE'S TOO COOL TO TRAVEL WITH HIS MUM AND SISTER!

D. IT COULD BE ANYWHERE IN THE WORLD, BUT HARRY TREATS THEM LIKE QUEENS AND MAKES SURE THEY'RE COMFY AND HAVING FUN.

7. Harry tries out for an Oscar-worthy role but loses out to another thespian. How does he react?

A. FIGURES IT WASN'T MEANT TO BE AND LOOKS FOR ANOTHER DOOR THAT MIGHT OPEN TO HIM SINCE HE ISN'T DOING THAT FILM.

B. CALLS THE DIRECTOR AND PLEADS.

C. TRASHES THE ACTOR WHO GOT THE ROLE VIA SOCIAL MEDIA.

D. TELLS ALL HIS FANS THAT THE FILM IS RUBBISH.

8. Hazza's in the mood for movie night. What does he watch?

A. *THE AMITYVILLE HORROR*

B. *SINGIN' IN THE RAIN*

C. *LOVE ACTUALLY*

D. *TO CATCH A THIEF*

9. Harry can go back in time and perform with any musician. Who would it be?

A. THE MONKEES

B. BOBBY DARIN

C. MADONNA

D. ELVIS

10. Harry's girlfriend breaks up with him, so he . . .

A. MAKES SNIDE REMARKS ABOUT HER ONLINE.

B. IMMEDIATELY HOOKS UP WITH THE NEXT GIRL HE SEES.

C. TAKES SOME DOWNTIME AND WRITES A SONG ABOUT IT WHERE HE LOOKS AT HIS MISTAKES AS WELL AS HERS.

D. HITS THE PARTY CIRCUIT FOR THREE MONTHS STRAIGHT.

How did you do?
Check your answers on page 95!

1-3 correct: You hardly know Harry.

4-6 correct: Only direction to go is up.

7-10 correct: You're a Styles stan!

CHAPTER 4

LOVE, HARRY STYLE

So, you might think there will be tons of juicy tidbits in this chapter, and we couldn't blame you. We all know DH has been linked to lots of different girls since he came into the public eye. It's been rather fun to watch as he is young. And scampy!

But remember, he's also a gentleman. So while there are sightings to report and a few quotes here and there, Harry generally does *not* kiss and tell. And out of respect for his chivalrous ways, we're just going to go surface level here.

Chivalry aside, there's another reason we won't deep dive: From the get-go, there have been rather rabid fans who say not-so-nice things to Hazza's dates. We wish we were joking, but we're not!

Harry and model Nadine Leopold dated for a bit in 2015, and the poor girl got so much hate. Even death threats! She said, "I got pictures sent to my apartment with my face crossed out. It affects your whole relationship because you think about that, and you're worried."

Then we had Camille Rowe, whom he dated for about a year. When they were first together, and she posted an Insta story that seemed to have his voice on it, fans went off the rails. One even said, "I'm gonna cry."

We've said this before, but it bears repeating: SUPPORTING>STALKING!

It's unwise, not to mention unsound, to be unkind, and we know Harry wouldn't want anyone behaving that way! So un-Harry-like. If the girls who do things like this think it will make them more attractive to DH, they should think again.

Also, speaking of his gentlemanliness, Harry has stayed friends with most of his former paramours. Camille, for one. Kendall Jenner, for another.

HERE'S THE SCOOP! ON HARRY AND KENDALL

Remember when we SCOOPed that Hazza stepped in to host *The Late Late Show* when James Corden's wife was giving birth? Well, Kendall Jenner was one of the guests. Even though they dated on and off for years, a source says, "Harry and Kendall are great friends and always have been." They proved it well and good as they played "Spill Your Guts or Fill Your Guts," a game where two contestants ask each other awkward questions. Harry had to ask Kendall which of her siblings was the best parent! AWKWARD. (She said Rob!) When Ms. Jenner asked DH which song from his first solo album was about her, he decided to "fill his guts" instead of answering!

See what we mean about Harry's gentlemanly reluctance to spill any beans? We guess he'd rather eat them. Regarding Kendall, though . . . we have a little feeling they aren't together because of impossible schedules—he on tour and her flying the world for fashion shows and shoots. Why do we think this? That source (probably a publicist, let's face it) also said, "They don't get to spend a lot of time together, but when they do, they always have a blast. It's an easy, super-chill friendship."

That certainly makes for a softer breakup than if there's a huge blowout fight, and also leaves room for possible reunions. We'll look at that in a moment. (Wink!)

We must admit, though, there is one ship that didn't exactly sail smoothly. Or, we suppose, dock smoothly. You know who we're talking about. Taylor.

The deets as we know them are thus: Harry and Taylor were introduced by Ed Sheeran, who's still friends with both of them. They went out of the gate running, taking tons of trips together (Utah, the Caribbean, and lots of places around the UK and NYC). He got her cupcakes for her birthday. They even had a snowmobile accident together. EEK! But one minute they were holding hands in Central Park, and the next, poof. After dating for just a few months, it was over. Harry was apparently embarrassed about how quickly they'd broken up because he'd been warned it wouldn't last.

At least they both got a lot of good music out of it. We know Swift's "I Knew You Were Trouble" and "Out of the Woods" (yikes again, re that snowmobile fracas) were about Hazza, and his "Two Ghosts" was (likely) about Taylor. We have a feeling from her lyrics—"Every day was a struggle/ Forget making plans for life"—that perhaps Taylor wanted to settle down and Harry did not. He was, after all, only nineteen!!

BUT WE HAVE BIGGER-PICTURE SCOOP!

Leave it to Dear Harry to make sure there was no (long-term) bad blood. He told Howard Stern he likes to look at the bigger picture and doesn't mind that she wrote songs about him. "I think about what it means to me to write a song about somebody else and for somebody else to do that, it's like flattering. Even if the song isn't that flattering, you still spent time on it."

You know, if this whole rock god/actor/evolved-artist thing doesn't work out, we think Harry could have a career in diplomacy.

But as mentioned, it's hard to have a relationship if you're in the public eye. It adds so much pressure to everything, because once the (rabid) fans find out, they're either shipping them so hard they want to know all the details, or upset it's not them and possibly unkind to the new gf. Total lunacy!

There's also tons of misinformation out there. If Harry is so much as hanging out with someone, everyone assumes she's a girlfriend. It's a little wack, even to the point where Harry has said, "The thing with that is, I do have friends—and I'd say that more than 90 percent of the people I get linked with are my friends. At the moment, it appears that I have, like, seven thousand girlfriends. It's just ridiculous."

On that, we're just going to make things easy with a simple list of (reported) actual girlfriends. And then move on!

2011: Caroline Flack, *X Factor* presenter

2012: Emily Ostilly, model

(Later in) 2012: Emily Atack, actor

(Ummm, even later in) 2012: Caggie Dunlop, reality TV actor

(Yet even later in) 2012 to early 2013: Taylor Swift (no wonder it didn't work long-term—Hazza needed some downtime!)

2013: Nicole Scherzinger, singer and *X Factor* judge

2013: Kimberly Stewart, rocker Rod Stewart's daughter

2013–2014: Kendall Jenner, model

2014: Erin Foster, model

2014–2015: Nadine Leopold, model

2015: Sara Sampaio, model (we're sensing another pattern here)

2015: Georgia Fowler, model

2015–2016: Kendall again!! (still a model last time we looked)

2017: Tess Ward, chef and food blogger (thank goodness for a slight change there)

2017–2018: Camille Rowe, model

So! There we have it. Our question isn't focused on why Harry has been dating around so much (he is in his twenties after all!), but on how none of these ladies have anything bad to say about him?! We can trace it back to . . . home.

His mum! Anne! She taught him manners and to be honest. So if he has those, even if he's not ready to settle down, how mad could a girl really get at him? He was raised with his sister by a single mum. He learned to be caring and a gentleman.

HERE'S THE SCOOP! ON HARRY'S MUM!

Before he was the world's knight in shining armor, he was his mum's. And he still dotes on her!

"Harry's a very romantic guy. If I'd had a particularly bad day at work, I'd come home to find he'd run me a bath and surrounded it with candles and even cooked me a meal. He just used to usher me out of the kitchen and say he'd got it all under control." He walked her down the aisle when she married his stepdad, who in 2017 sadly passed away. He told *Rolling Stone*, "it's kind of felt like—protect Mom at all costs. . . . My mom is very strong. She has the greatest heart. [Her house in Cheshire] is where I want to go when I want to spend some time."

We've always said you can tell someone is a great guy if he treats his mum well.

Not to say Harry doesn't focus on his girlfriends. In fact, he sometimes thinks too much. He used to research dates! But then said, "I'm not going to do that anymore, it's impossible to go in without a perception of someone, and you've never met them, and I started feeling like that was wrong and weird."

We can kind of understand why anyone would research, though, and especially Hazza. It's such pressure anytime he goes out with anyone when the whole world is watching! Everyone talks about everything he does! He's great friends with Adele, and recently they went on holiday with James Corden and family, and the rumor mill was churning out Hadele stories. But they're just friends. And he and Kendall . . . well, who knows. They hung out after the Brit Awards 2020 so maybe things are rekindling. Or not. But can you imagine having every move watched?

Regarding rumors, DH said, "Some of them are funny. Some of them are ridiculous. Some of them are annoying. I don't want to be one of those people that complains about the rumors. I never like it when a celebrity goes on Twitter and says: 'This isn't true!' It is what it is; I tend not to do that. The only time it gets really annoying is that if you get into a relationship and you get into a place where you really like someone and then things are being written in the papers that affect them and how they see you. Then it can get annoying."

Perhaps like with Camille Rowe? Harry was reportedly upset about their breakup, and you can feel that in many songs from *Fine Line*, like "Cherry," as well as the title track. *Variety* felt it wasn't so much that Hazza was hurt as it was "an album about romantic ambivalence, really, which is a perfectly fine subject for a twenty-five-year-old who's still sowing some oats to settle in on."

Either way, it's got to be terrible having all your deets out in the world.

So let's give Harry some room.

We promise not to speculate on actual romances, but up next, we'll play our favorite game of who could be the perfect date for Dear Harry!

SCOOP! EXTRA

Below we play one of our favorite games ever! Our best guesses on

who ... what ... where & why

would be a great date for Harry!

Kendall Jenner

WHAT: A twelve-course meal at a James Beard Award–winning restaurant

WHERE: Maybe Wolvesmouth at the Wolvesden?

WHY: So . . . they seem like they might still like to hang out, and after that adorable but disgusting game of "Spill or Fill" they had to play while he was hosting James Corden's *The Late Late Show*, we feel they deserve a nice meal together!

Emily Adams Bode

WHAT: Fashion Show

WHERE: Milan

WHY: Just to get us off the model path for a moment, we thought pretty fashion designer Emily would be a good way to go. Her label, Bode, is made from globally sourced antique fabrics. So cool!

Carly Stein

WHAT: A picnic

WHERE: Tuscany, Italy

WHY: Founder of Beekeeper's Naturals, a wellness company that makes a throat spray boasting bee propolis, an immunity superfood containing over three hundred ingredients. Plus, she's cute as the bee's knees!

Zendaya

WHAT: A hike, a walk, a movie, an acting class, or even cooking together

WHERE: Anywhere

WHY: She's Zendaya. We love her! She's amazing, not to mention stunning. Enough said.

Cressida Bonas

WHAT: Theater night

WHERE: London's West End

WHY: Well, she almost got hitched with the other Prince Harry, and like our Hazza, is a budding actor. And adorable.

Emma Watson

WHAT: Dinner and a Women's March for Equality

WHERE: London, NYC, you name it!

WHY: Beautiful Emma is an active feminist, and Harry supports her #HeForShe campaign!

Saumya

WHAT: A farm visit

WHERE: India

WHY: Saumya cofounded Kheyti, which uses its "Greenhouse-in-a-Box" to help small farms "grow seven times more food using 90% less water." Basically, she's both gorgeous and saving the world!

Lily James

WHAT: Sunday brunch

WHERE: A cool London pub

WHY: We are now quoting ourselves, but "we will keep listing her for everyone until she's off the market as we just think she seems cool and fun!"

Liza Koshy

WHAT: Dancing

WHERE: On his stage

WHY: She makes us gasp for breath laughing, and with Harry's excellent sense of humor, he'd surely have a blast with Lizzzzzza.

Emilia Clarke

WHAT: A day of play

WHERE: London

WHY: She's fun and funny, and seems to have a Harry-like ability to laugh at herself. We promise you, not taking yourself too seriously is a gift. Plus, she's had some health scares, so she's all about gratitude for what she's got. Personality match made!!

CHAPTER 5

STAYING SANE WITH STYLE

*T*oo much adoration can turn ugly. As we saw in the last chapter, some fabids (rabid fans) get a wee bit carried away and start trolling any girl with whom Harry hangs. But did you know some fabids make it hard for him to have just plain old mates?

Remember the whole Larry Stylinson thing, where just because DH and Louis Tomlinson were such great friends that people began to speculate that they were an item? Now, this is not to say that it would've been bad if they *had* been an item, but our point is that Hazza cannot make ONE MOVE without intense scrutiny. It would mess with any friendship, and it did mess with Louis and Harry's! There would even be fan fiction where someone would take a pic of the group where one of them is kissing a girl, and Photoshop her out so it looked like Harry and Louis were smooching.

Come ON, fabids? Even when 1D denied the rumors, they refused to believe it. It made Harry and Louis reluctant to even stand next to one another, much less behave like the good mates they were. Eventually it actually put a wedge between their friendship.

Every move Hazza made was picked apart. Even another celebrity got in on it. Harry became great friends with Nick Grimshaw, but some comedian (that we'd never heard of, so maybe he's just trying to get his name out there) just had to razz them about it. He told *The Sun*, "Like Nick is my age, and Harry is about eighteen and they play frisbee together—it's really weird."

Pardon us? Why is he even commenting on their friendship?

Not that it's any of the comedian's business, but there are plenty of people who find DH more

mature than his age. Much more! Tom Hull—
his close friend and coproducer who has been
with Harry day in, day out working together on
his solo albums, and therefore a more reliable
source (and born in 1982 so even older than Mr.
Grimshaw of 1984)—says, "He's got this wise-
beyond-his-years timelessness about him." And for
Harry's part, he likes to learn from those who may
have more experience, saying, "It's nice to hang
out with people who are maybe in a later stage of
what I'm going through right now."

Perhaps Mr. Comedian could take a few pointers
on friendship from Hazza himself. We know how
inclusive Harry is and how he would never shame
anyone for any kind of relationship. Seems much
more mature than calling others weird.

But poor Harry. It's hard to form relationships
while inside the fishbowl of fame, n'est-ce pas?

Even worse, there have been truly frightening
ramifications of fame: Harry had once spotted a
homeless man sleeping outside on a wet night,

and of course, DH felt terrible for him. He offered the guy money, but the man said he couldn't take money for religious reasons. Incredibly sweet, Harry showed up the next day with food for him. The man asked Harry to go to a restaurant to eat with him. Hazza politely declined, at which point the man got a strange look on his face. Suddenly, about four times a week, he began showing up at Harry's local pub one to two minutes after his arrival. Harry knew he was being followed. The stranger then began showing up at his house and even found him running in Regent's Park to ask for the money Harry initially offered. YIKES!

Luckily, Harry hired some more security and the man was found guilty of stalking.

As you can see, the upsides of fame—money, power, access—definitely come with some liabilities. That access itself can be tricky.

Many performers get rather full of themselves and become *très* annoying to be around. You've heard of those wild contracts some stars have for the venue when they're performing, no? Demanding everything from a new toilet seat for every venue (Madonna), one hundred white doves and twenty white kittens (OMG Mariah!!!!), Versace towels (Kanye), and, more simply, instructions on how to use any electronics there (the Rolling Stones).

Not Harry, though. When One Direction arrived for a *Cosmopolitan* photoshoot—the first all-male cover, ever—editor Louise Court said they were the opposite of difficult. They arrived early and made tea! That must be another first.

Another problem with that access? Well, lots of people throwing themselves at you. Sounds nice at first, but if you're in love, not so much. Even worse, if you're in love but lonely from being on the road for months, one might get tempted. We are kind of wondering if perhaps that's what happened between Harry and Camille Rowe. We know he was sad when they split, and his lyrics, "there's no one to blame but the drink and my wandering hands," in the song "Falling" hint at that kind of mistake!

There's guilt on top of the pain, making the

situation even sadder. Ugh!

But from the get-go, Harry has always taken things in stride and been optimistic. His lighthearted humor is why he's so adored and he's cheerful about his fame, too! He knows that it's both funny and ephemeral.

So when he opened the *Love On Tour* launch concert, the first words out of his mouth were, "Good evening, my name's Harry."

In keeping with the self-deprecation of the evening, after singing the song "To Be So Lonely," he was laughing as he asked the audience, "Why when I called myself an arrogant son of a %@$&★!, why is that when you sang the loudest?"

We're guessing because although you should be arrogant, Harry, you are kind and thoughtful. Well done.

Sometimes fame does get to him, though. Like when someone published the location of his pad in London. Whoa. What a thing to do! Can you imagine? Harry, however, took the advice of his friend James Corden, who quoted former British prime minister Benjamin Disraeli: "Never complain, never explain."

Hmmm, we're very glad that motto is working for Harry. And it's quite clear it is. However, it also seems to be a modus operandi for the British Royal Family.

Speaking of odd, we do have an utterly bizarre SCOOP! One day Harry wasn't well while traveling a California freeway and had to pull over to vomit, as one does. Now the next part is so gross we can barely print it! A fabid is said to have collected it and tried to sell it on eBay. Blech! Always with the sense of humor, DH said: "My mom actually sent me, like, an eBay link to my own puke, which was very interesting to receive on a Tuesday morning."

That is just a new level of stanning that we don't want to think about further. What we *will* say is that this kind of lunacy makes it necessary to take precautions. So precautions Harry takes!

When his mum, Anne, married his stepfather, Robin Twist, in 2012, the details on the venue were kept quiet so that One Directioners wouldn't stampede and ruin the wedding. In a brilliant logistical move, they even got a decoy bus filled with fake wedding guests to lead the fabids eighty miles away at the Doncaster Racecourse!

We're so happy for them that they were able to have peace at their wedding. And adorable DH stayed by his mum's side all night. Being so close with her, it's no wonder Harry has such a good head on his shoulders, especially for someone so young.

Harry could easily get lost, but he doesn't. And according to a close family friend, there's one answer to how he's managed to stay clear of the quagmire.

"Family," said a *Late Late Show* executive

producer. "It comes from his mom, Anne. She brought him and his sister up incredibly well. Harry would choose boring over exciting. . . . There is more chance of me going to Mars next week than there is of Harry having some sort of addiction."

Harry couldn't agree more. In that interview with Paul McCartney we SCOOPed for you, they spoke about the pitfalls of fame. It's all clear.

Harry: "If you can step outside of the craziness and appreciate it for the fact that it's extraordinary, see it as this amazing thing for a second, it's alright. If you just think that's how life is, that's when you lose touch. It's good to have people who can tell you you're an idiot and tell you when you're wrong. I think that's as important as having people geeing you up sometimes. Going home is probably always the answer."

PM: "Yeah I'll go along with that. In fact, I'll come home with you Harry."

HS: "My mum would love it."

As would all of Holmes Chapel. Enjoy!

73

HILARIOUS HARRY:
⬇ FUNNY MOMENTS WITH HAZZA ⬇

1D playing dodgeball on *The Late Late Show with James Corden* and Harry jokes, "The last five years with this band has all been in preparation for this game."

Hazza excitedly tossing a water bottle in the air, thinking a fan would catch it, but it hit them in the face. Harry was mortified and froze, hand over mouth in shock for several moments.

Harry telling Howard Stern how he was robbed at knifepoint on Valentine's Day and said, "I guess that's what you get for being single these days."

Harranigans: "Eating toast in the shower is the ultimate multitask."

 More Harranigans: "Man cannot live by coffee alone, but he will give it a damn good try."

At a concert in Boston, Harry quipping, "Boston, are you having a good time? Because if not, we're fired."

 Hazza razzing a fan for not having a phone, saying, "It's 2015!!" His bandmate had to yell, "Harry, she's five!"

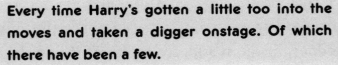 Every time Harry's gotten a little too into the moves and taken a digger onstage. Of which there have been a few.

 A fan handing over a box of homemade cookies, and Harry turning to the crowd and shouting, "Why didn't you all make cookies?!?!?"

CHAPTER 6

PRINCE HARRY

By now, we've made it abundantly clear what we think of Harry Styles. He's got one of the best personalities out there—kind, thoughtful, inclusive, empathetic. The fact that he's uber-talented, handsome, hilarious, and so much fun to watch is like icing on the cake. Basically, he's a prince.

Which is good, because as mentioned in the last chapter, Britain could use another one right now. We jest, but truly, you can't have too much kindness in the world. Even one of the tracks on *Fine Line* is called "Treat People with Kindness."

We always see that kindness with Harry. Some of those ways we've already mentioned. The way he handled Zayn's negative comments about

One Direction, his diplomacy regarding former girlfriends, helping the fan who had fainted at a show, and how he handled it like a pro when some fans threw bottles at him onstage by grasping his head and then moving on as if nothing happened.

Here's another **SCOOP!** on Harry's mum! We can tell you that Anne was not pleased when someone beaned him with a can of Red Bull! Even though Hazza didn't react, she had her son's back (and head). She tweeted under the wonderful moniker Miss Twist: "No harm done . . . This time . . . Unless you're on a sports field is it acceptable to throw things at people?! I think not."

Here's a princely proverb: Don't mess with the queen mums. They'll have your head!

Harry has been using his shows and his fame for good works since the get-go. He understands his privilege and wants to use it to help others.

At his shows, he happily waves Black Lives Matter flags and Pride flags, and has had an End Gun Violence sticker on his guitar. "I want to make people feel comfortable being whatever they want to be," DH told *Rolling Stone*. "Maybe at a show you can have a moment of knowing that you're not alone. I'm aware that as a white male, I don't go through the same things as a lot of the people that come to the shows. I can't claim that I know what it's like, because I don't. So I'm not trying to say, 'I understand what it's like.' I'm just trying to make people feel included and seen."

While he normally stays off social media unless there's an album to promote, he's also tweeted support of the 2017 Women's March in Washington, DC, writing: "Yesterday was amazing. Unity and love. Always equal. H."

But he keeps a tight lid on social media

for a reason. "It's the most incredible way to communicate closely with people, but not as well as in person." There's that good sense his mum instilled in him!

But you know Harry has always been involved in philanthropy. In Chapter One, we gushed over how he and Liam became ambassadors for Trekstock, and how One Direction donated proceeds from "One Way or Another" to Comic Relief.

Hazza puts his money where his mouth is! To support Lifewater's World Water Day in 2015, DH donated through drop4drop to sponsor water wells in India. Then in 2016, he chopped off those long locks of his and donated them to Little Princess Trust, which gives wigs to sick children who have lost their hair, surely brightening up a little one's day! When he played small shows to launch his first solo album at the Troubadour and The Garage, all proceeds went to charities, including the LA organization Safe Place for Youth, which provides resources and solutions for homeless youth, and again to the Little Princess Trust. When Hazza finished his first solo tour, $1.2 million of ticket sales went to over sixty-two charities around the globe. To top it all off, he promoted environmentalism the whole tour through reducing plastic bottle waste and recycling!

And that's what makes him beautiful.

While Harry's concerts are indeed the perfect platform for making a difference, he's also tweeted for good more than once. Hazza supported the March for Our Lives campaign, tweeting, "I just signed the @AMarch4OurLives petition, and you should too. H," as well as the HeForShe gender equality campaign, saying, "I'm supporting @UN_Women and @EmWatson in #HeForShe. As should you."

Harry being Harry, though, he keeps it humble. For him, being a feminist is a no-brainer, explaining that it doesn't mean anything bad toward men; it just means equality! Speaking with *Rolling Stone*, he quipped, "Of course men and women should be equal. I don't want a lot of credit for being a feminist. It's pretty simple. I think the ideals of feminism are pretty straightforward."

In keeping with his humble and candid attitude, the small things he does also show his altruism. While Harry was still in 1D, they performed at a US *X Factor* show, and tweeted a consolation to Fifth Harmony when they didn't win: "You were amazing. You're going to be great. Have a good night. xxx."

These little everyday things show Harry's true colors. And those colors are brilliant.

Another clue that Hazza is a gem is how much other celebs like him. We've talked about his friendships with James Corden, Nick Grimshaw, and Adele, but there's more! Ed Sheeran, who is also a close mate, touted Harry's giving nature, saying, "We were in LA . . . and he had a day off. [Harry] spent two or three grand on Domino's pizza and drove around giving them out to homeless people." Purely princely!

Also on the Hurrah Harry list are Emma
Roberts, Rita Ora, Meghan Trainor, John Legend,
Rihanna, Elton John (who knows clothes!), Chris
Martin (who called Hazza "the most handsome
man in the world"), and Kesha. The latter singer/
songwriter raved, saying, "He's a beautiful thing,
isn't he? I actually gave him an award at some
show, so I got to give him a little squeeze. [His
hair] smells like roses and tropical lotions mixed
with butterflies."

We think we can safely say we agree with all of
that! What's amazing to us is that with such fervent
admirers, he keeps his ego in check. He knows he
comes from a place of privilege.

"It's not about me trying to champion the cause,
because I'm not the person to do that," he said
to *Rolling Stone*. "It's just about not ignoring it,
I guess. I was a little nervous to do that because
the last thing I wanted was for it to feel like I was
saying, 'Look at me! I'm the good guy!'"

We understand, Harry. You don't want to toot

your own horn. But you *are* the good guy!!

Another way Harry showed that he's 100 percent golden is with the song "Sign of the Times." Get this: He wrote it from the viewpoint of a mother giving birth, but with a complication. She's told her baby will survive but she will not. It's heartrending, beautiful, and an amazing exploration of the bond between mother and child, especially with all the chaos happening on earth.

Dear Harry said to NPR, "Yeah, I think we were thinking about—there's a lot of bad stuff going on in the world. And it's not the last time that we will be in a place like that. I think the way that we receive information all the time now, it's really difficult to ignore that stuff—and I think it would have been weird for me to write an album and not acknowledge that there's anything bad going on in the world. And I think we were writing it from a place of—you have five minutes to say, 'It's going to be all right.'"

Okay, call us batty, but what other twenty-three-year-old (his age at the time) could put himself in that headspace? Wethinks none. He is a wildly good egg.

WE'LL LEAVE THIS CHAPTER WITH SOME PRINCELY SCOOP!

Recently, we've also come to the conclusion that some of the best princes shy away from the title (hint: Sussex). Like when Harry turned down the role of Eric in *The Little Mermaid*. Instead of saying it wasn't his cup of tea, he said that he wanted to focus on his music for the time being, making sure to compliment the project with the rejoinder that "everyone involved in it was amazing. So I think it's going to be great."

Even though Harry turned down the role of a prince, we can assure you he's one anyway!

CHAPTER 7

FUTURE STYLES

*L*ast chapter, we noted that Prince Harry declined to play *The Little Mermaid*'s Eric to concentrate on music. And concentrate he did.

The album *Fine Line* is proof positive. It's funky, soulful, sometimes poppy, sometimes folksy. And pure Harry. We haven't been able to stop listening. *Rolling Stone* writes that "Golden" is like "'70s SoCal rock," "Watermelon Sugar" is as delish as it sounds, "Cherry" is otherworldly, and "Falling" is a moving ballad. We could go on, but if you haven't already, you *must* put it on your playlist.

We're almost afraid to tout the *Love On Tour* because we all know how that's going to go. It will sell out like hotcakes, and we want to be sure we get seats! Ticketmaster actually crashed during presale tickets. One rattled fan tweeted a screenshot of a screen message saying she was number two thousand in the queue!!

You know that's what happened with his first solo tour, *Harry Styles: Live on Tour*, and people went ballistic.

Ever the sweetheart, he tweeted a note saying, "I am overwhelmed, thank you. If I don't get to see you this tour (first solo tour), I'll come back around next year if you'll have me. Love, H."

The lucky ones who got tickets put on quite the show themselves. At Madison Square Garden, fans went so wild during "Kiwi" that the floor actually started to shake! Rob Sheffield of *Rolling Stone* said, "I've been seeing shows there since the 1980s, but I'd never seen that happen before. (The only other time? His second night.) His bandmates admit they feared for their lives, but Harry relished it. 'To me, the greatest thing about the tour was that the room became the show. . . . I'm just a boy, standing in front of a room, asking them to bear with him.'"

Whether or not you saw Harry last tour, are going to this one, or both, you know that it's a treat as Harry was a born performer. It was always evident, even in the 1D days. Hazza was always completely comfortable onstage, and his chatting between tracks was spot-on. To alternately make people LOL and then make them jam out? Yes, please!

It's been pretty great for Harry, too! At the *Fine Line* launch concert, after that adorable "Good morning. My name is Harry," he said, "This is my wonderful band. For the last two years, after the first song, playing in front of anyone, I've had to say I only have ten songs. I have more than ten songs now. We're gonna play a few tonight."

We couldn't be happier for him.

However, we can't promise everything is just going to go in one direction (that was the *last* pun, we promise) from here on out. As we know, Dear Harry likes to keep things interesting.

Harry has already been in three—count 'em, three—Gucci campaigns. We must say he looks smashing in them, too. Two of them were for Gucci tailoring, with the first one set in a fish and chips shop in St. Albans, where he is in a New Marseille jacket with an embroidered collar and holding a chicken. Our eyes popped out.

For the second campaign, he found himself in a place called Villa Lante, just north of Rome, in stunning sixteenth-century Renaissance gardens. If that weren't gorgeous enough, according to *British Vogue*, Dear Harry romped around in "coloured jacquards, patches, checkered prints, unusual proportions and a particularly fetching pair of lilac tailored trousers." In a veritable feast for the eyes, he's holding adorable farm pets such as baby goats, lambs, and piglets!

The clothes are like artwork, which we know about because one of our favorite artists works with Gucci! Her name is Helen Downie, and her paintings are like magical, glamorous netherworlds. Gucci discovered her when she started posting her work on Instagram under the moniker "Unskilled

Worker." But don't let the name fool you–she is highly, incredibly skilled! In an interview with *artnet News*, she said, "I think I'm always trying to get back to my childhood; to get back to the wonder I felt as a seven-year-old and to take people with me." It all fits Harry to a tee, no?

Then there was the third, the fragrance campaign for Mémoire d'une Odeur. This time it was ethereal pics of Hazza and fellow beautiful people picnicking amongst the ruins of Canale Monterano, in what used to be a commune— again in Italy, which is always good in our book. It's all so lovely one can't help but wish one was there, too.

On top of all this, Harry also cochaired the 2019 Met Gala alongside Gucci's Alessandro Michele, Lady Gaga, Serena Williams, and of course, Anna Wintour. The theme was "Camp: Notes on Fashion," a fun and feisty motif in which DH thrived. No surprise. Fun and feisty, thy name is Harry!

There seems to be no end to the roles he can play!

We also have a feeling there's going to be a couple more film roles in his future. Remember, he got the part in *Dunkirk* on his own chops, not because he was a celebrity musician. Director Christopher Nolan praised Harry's performance, and before its release, he told *Business Insider*, "I'm very excited for people to see what he has done in the film. I think it's truthful, and it's a very tough role he's playing, too."

The writer Jason Guerrasio said, "Styles delivers a riveting performance. And for a movie with limited dialogue, he gets a large part of the lines that are spoken."

We're so excited to see what comes next for Hazza, which we're sure will be full of wonderful surprises. Especially with his princely kindness, which we rate as his best trait, closely followed by his sense of fun and easygoing charm. That kindness comes naturally to him is clear.

AND LIKE A CHERRY ON TOP, WE HAVE A BIT OF LAST-MINUTE KINDNESS SCOOP!

Harry believes in karma, not surprising given how he both has and gives off such good karma! He told Chelsea Handler, "I feel like anyone who says, 'I'm spiritual' sounds a little wanky. But yeah, I definitely consider myself to be more spiritual than religious. I'm not super tied-in to certain rules, but I think it's naïve to say nothing exists, and there's nothing above us or more powerful than us. I think that's a little narrow-minded." He added, "I definitely think there's something, that it's not just us. It's kind of crazy to think that it's just us."

Hear! Hear! Love is all around the globe, especially when Harry cheers the place!

THE HURRAH HARRY ROLES OF THE FUTURE

Before we close shop, here's an extra SCOOP! We've imagined the songs, roles, and fashion campaigns in Dear Harry's stellar future.

★ Harry should do a rendition of David Bowie's "Golden Years." Perfect for him.

★ Harry as Hugh Grant's replacement as prime minister in *Love Actually 2.*

★ Eventually he and Taylor Swift should collaborate. If Stevie Nicks and Lindsey Buckingham could do it after their breakup, so can Hazza and Taylor!

★ Harry should portray Paul McCartney in a biopic of his life.

★ Ditto with David Bowie.

★ Hazza and Chris Martin should collaborate on a rock opera.

★ Harry is too sweet to play stern Mr. Darcy in Jane Austen's *Pride and Prejudice*, but he'd make an excellent Mr. Bingley.

★ He would also do Jane proud as Mr. Knightley in *Emma*.

★ Harry Styles must cover Elvis Presley's "Blue Suede Shoes" while wearing a pair, preferably from Gucci.

★ 007. Of course!

★ Perhaps he could snag the role of his alter ego Prince Harry if *The Crown* makes it past the '90s!

★ Given his excellent impression of Mick Jagger on *SNL*, we'd love for Dear Harry to cover "Wild Horses," as it's just so Harry . . .

WRITE YOUR OWN SCOOP!

Harry supports lots of charities and causes.
What three charities would you most like to
support and why?

1 _____

_____

_____

2 _____

_____

_____

3 _____

_____

_____

ANSWER KEY

HOW WELL DO YOU KNOW HAZZA?

1. C, 2. D, 3. A, 4. D, 5. B, 6. D,
7. A, 8. D, 9. D, 10. C

**HELP US PICK THE
NEXT ISSUE OF**

HERE'S HOW TO VOTE:

Go to

www.ReadScoop.com

**to cast your vote for
who we should
SCOOP! next.**